Our Invisible Cries in the Dark

Letters to Fathers From the Daughters They've Forgotten

Angela Carr Patterson

Angela Carr Patterson

Copyright © Angela Carr Patterson, 2015
All Rights Reserved

Published by:
Oasis Promotions Publishing
4611 Hardscrabble Road, Suite 193
Columbia, SC 29229
ISBN-13: 978-1517475444
ISBN-10: 1517475449ISBN:
ISBN-13:

No part of this publication may be reproduced or transmitted in any form by any means, electronic or mechanical, including photocopy, recording, or any infor-mation without prior approval from the publisher.

The information provided in this book is designed to provide helpful information on the subject discussed and provide motivation to our readers. This book is not meant to be used, to diagnose or treat any psychological condition. It is sold with the understanding that the author and publisher is not engaged to render any type of psychological, legal, or any other kind of professional advice. The content is the sole expression and opinion of its author. Neither the publisher nor the author shall be liable for any physical, psycho-logical, emotional, financial or commercial damages. You are responsible for your own choices, actions and results.

Dedication

To the fatherless daughters who stood in your power and shared your truth in your let-ters. I salute your bravery and your courage. No longer will your voice be silent and invisible. You deserve to be seen, be heard and be loved. You are a beautiful divine master piece beyond your fatherlessness.

To the fathers of the world who simply couldn't and didn't know how to connect with your daughter, I dedicate this book to you. I ask that you open your heart and make a new choice today. I salute you and encourage you to love and connect with your daughter in a more powerful and complete way.

To the members of The Fatherless Daughters Network: May we continue this journey of elevating the awareness of impact of fatherlessness on a female's life and providing the journey of love, acceptance and forgiveness.

Acknowledgments

To the girls who attended The 2015 Fatherless Girls Summit. You inspired this work and we will forever be grateful for your courage.

To India Phillips for the beautiful poem, "A Fatherless Daughter Cry."

To Curt Thomas for your powerful message to the girls at The 2015 Fatherless Girls Summit. We will never forget that moving message. We also thank you for this heart touching Foreword.

To all of the volunteers, sponsors, speakers, entertainers and staff of The Fatherless Girls Summit. It's because of you that this book was able to become a reality. Thanks for your support, time and money.

To my children and grandchildren, you have been my greatest inspiration and have be-lieved in me when I couldn't believe in myself.

To my husband, Bill: Thank you for creating a loving space for me to grow and expand. Thank you for simply standing with me as I live my dreams. I love you for being who you are, for loving me unconditionally, and for being my divine right man!

Table Of Contents

Dedication	iii
Acknowledgments	iv
Table Of Contents	v
Foreword	vi
The Fatherless Daughter Cry	ix
Introduction	1
Chapter One : On Fatherless Daughters	7
Chapter Two : Letters To Daddy	14
Chapter Three : Fatherless Women Un-Mute	47
Chapter Four : A Father's Love	73
Chapter Five : The Journey	82
Chapter Six : Where Do We Go From Here?	91
About The Author	96

Foreword

Who can wipe the tear that will not fall? Who can hear the silent cry that screams from the depths of so many fatherless girls' heart around the world?

Our Invisible Cries in the Dark by Angela Carr Patterson has made such an attempt. Angela's collection of letters personally handwritten from fatherless girls is a masterpiece. Angela Carr Patterson is and has been an inspiration to the masses for years. This book is nothing short of an example of her dedication to empowering fatherless girls.

As an admirer of Angela's work and dedication to her passion for fatherless girls, I antici-pate that the reader will find rapport and strength in these passionate handwritten letters from the young girls who were in attendance at The Fatherless Girls Summit hosted by Angela in summer of 2015. The reader will be able to feel the energy from the fatherless girls who wrote them from their hearts, tears, loneliness, and forgiveness.

I challenge the role of fatherhood with the men who will read this book. I am not making an attempt to point a

finger at you or cast shame upon you. However, I challenge you brother to find it within your heart to ask for the strength to look beyond whatever issue that maybe hindering you from being there for your daughter. Many of us men may feel misunderstood, embarrassed, helpless, or even inadequate to be a part of their lives. I understand that sometimes many, not all, mothers make it hard for you, as a father, to get passed your own personal hurt from the unsuccessful relationship with her (mother). The weight of not being there for your daughter maybe heavy for you to bear sometimes. However, let me assure you, your absence in her life is even heavier! However, I strongly believe that "where there is a will, there is a way!"
If you are a father of a young daughter, your role of fatherhood will never be the same after reading these letters. These letters will be like arrows piercing the deepest part of your soul. My brother, your daughters need you, not just your money or your gifts but you! They need your love. They need your kisses. They need your hugs. They need to be affirmed by you, their father, that they are indeed loved. They need to hear it from you that they should be respected as queens. Most of all…they need to hear that they are yours!

While attending Angela Carr Patterson's The Fatherless Girls summit, I personally wit-nessed the hurt, pain, tears, disappointments, and even some hatred for absent fathers. However, what was more amazing to me was the resurrection of respect, love, self-esteem, and forgiveness from the young girls after they heard from Angela and her staff. Angela shared her own personal heartfelt story. She gave the young girls hope, inspira-tion, strategies, but most of all she gave them her, she was the example!

This is my hope for you, the reader, after you read this book. May you also feel the same emotions as you strive day by day to be the daughter/father that God has intended for you to be. With God's help, you will be strengthening to be the daughter, sister, mother, or grandmother that He has called you to be. Angela's work with confronting the issue of fatherless girls will positively impact generations to come.

Curt Thomas
Professional Speaker/Trainer
Keynote Speaker at The 2015 Fatherless Girls Summit
www.curtthomasspeaks.com

Our Invisible Cries In The Dark

The Fatherless Daughter Cry

I come from a family of great potential,
a family of hurt and pain.
A family who feels no one understands us,
and we wonder if they even know our name.
We are princesses,
We are beautiful,
although, we rarely get told.
Our lives are like puzzles,
incomplete,
oh, because we're missing a piece.
We're missing our first loves to show us
exactly who and exactly how to love.
to be there to tell us,
it's going to be okay.
That we didn't need that knuckle head anyways.
We'll never know how it feels to be tucked in at night
to be told that our worth is beyond our sight.
We're missing that piece,
that very important piece.
That piece is called Daddy.
That piece is gone from us, way too soon.
Will our incomplete puzzle ever be complete?
I'm a part of this family,
we're called the fatherless,
and we're girls who do not understand.
Does he love me?
I think.
Does he care?
I hope.
Maybe one day,
he'll show.
Daddy, where are you?
Your little girl needs you.

Angela Carr Patterson

Oh, will you ever know?
I'm a part of this family,
we're called the fatherless
and we're girls who don't understand,
So we try and make our own plans
Plans that we hope can fill this hole,
so deep inside of our souls.
I am fatherless, a fatherless girl.
A girl with a missing piece.
I have many sisters in this great big world,
and we need each other greatly!

By India Phillips

Introduction

I wish I could say that the words Fatherless Daughter didn't exist. Because it does. I wish it wasn't true that millions of girls will go to bed tonight without as much as a good night kiss from their daddy because he's nowhere to be found. But, it is true.

I wish that I could say that I didn't personally experience this incredibly painful hole in my soul from not having my father be there for me. But the truth is, he wasn't there and his absence left an incomprehensible pain and ache in my soul.

We all have a biological father but when the term fatherless is used it means that the father figure is just not present in the daughter's life. He may be unavailable, unattached or absent. Perhaps he died, may have run away or maybe he's physically present but not attentive and caring. Whatever the reason for a father not being present in his daughter's life, this one key missing element will have many negative consequences as she develops and grows in to adolescence and adulthood.

My story began when my mother and father, met, were married then separated during the time my mom became pregnant with me. They later divorced. I never had the pleasure of growing up knowing my father and having a relationship with him. As I became an adult, I went in search to find him with the hopes that I would finally become a daddy's girl. I did find my father. But, becoming daddy's little girl never became my reality.

I spent years hoping and wishing that my father-daughter-relationship would eventually blossom into a beautiful experience. Only to discover that my father was not capable of such a relationship.

Yet, the truth remained that I wanted so desperately to be daddy's little princess. I longed for his protection, for his provision, his presence and his praise. The thing I missed the most from not having a father around was the feeling of having someone to protect me. Someone who would stand up for me. In many ways today, I still long for that feeling of being protected.

For years, I struggled to make my life work. I struggled to have a healthy sense of self-worth, self-value or self-love. I struggled in my relationship men and my relationship with money. Because as fatherless daughters, how we do love is how we do money.

My invisible cries in the darkness of my soul went unheard because they were silenced by the pain of rejection and the insurmountable pain of feeling unwanted and unloved by my father.

I remember feeling a sense of loss and not belonging to anyone or anything. I couldn't understand why I felt so alone and as if my life had no real meaning. I later understood that my feelings came from my lack of identity. I didn't know who I was.

We get our identity through our paternal relationship. If that relationship doesn't exist or if it is flawed in anyway, we will experience deep trauma in many areas of our lives.

Emotional and psychological trauma has been defined as the result of extraordinarily stressful events that shatter your sense of security, making you feel helpless and vulnerable in a dangerous world. Lord knows, this is how I felt so many times in my life. Even as a woman, I felt a helpless lack of security and vulnerability with no one to protect me.

This loneliness and fear followed me for years. These feelings dictated the choices I made in my life and many were not in my best interest. It was when my marriage of sixteen years ended, that I began to seek help. I needed to find out why my life had ended up in such a deep, dark desolate space.

My Journey to being is what I call my healing process. It took years on this Journey for me to begin to heal my daddy wounds, to heal from my broken marriage and awaken to the truth of who I was as a woman. I wish that I could say it was easy. Because it wasn't. But it was simple.

I finally made peace with the truth that my father couldn't give me what I wanted and needed. I also recognized that if I was going to be free from this hole in my soul that I needed to forgive him and allow my broken heart to heal.

As I said before, it took years for me to finally redefine my life beyond my fatherlessness. It took a lot of work for me to understand this journey of love, acceptance and forgiveness. Yet, it was a journey I had to take in order for me to be free.

Today, I spend my time helping women and girls free themselves from the shackles of their daddy wounds, shatter the shame and actualize the power of self-love to create success in their lives.

I do this through my ground breaking work, "The Journey to Being Process™," designed to help fatherless girls and women heal their daddy wounds through a Journey of love, acceptance and forgiveness.

Little did I know that my fatherlessness would open an entire new world for me and so many women and girls around the globe. The driving force behind my work is that I never want any woman or girl to walk around with a hole in her soul because of her daddy wounds, or from any wound, for that matter.

This book was written to elevate the awareness of the negative impact an absent father can have on his daughter's life.

Our Invisible Cries in The Dark is not a book about blame. It's about giving women and girls a voice that had been silenced and unheard far too long. It's about telling the truth. It's about shattering the shame and taking a step in the direction to heal and forgive. This book was also birthed to give voice to the silent cries of girls and women who once held a belief that said, "I am invisible and do not exist in my daddy's eyes."

Truth of the matter is, some fathers don't know how to love their daughters. They abandon them, use them, abuse them, and manipulate them. There's nothing anyone can do to change such fathers. That's just who they are.

But we can change how we feel inside and how we respond to this uncaring behavior of our fathers. We can share our stories to help each other know and understand that we are not alone. And we can change our fate and make it not just bearable, but BETTER all together! The women and girls in this book are on their way to making it better. That's for sure!

Chapter One

On Fatherless Daughters

Pope John XXIII once said: "It is easier for a father to have children than for children to have a real father."

It is not easy to cope with being a fatherless daughter. As females, we crave to be loved, cared for, and cherished by those who brought us into life.

Listen to me: If this is your reality, know that you are not alone. More women and girls are fatherless than you can imagine.

Angela Carr Patterson

A recent study from Lisa Mancini and Professor Briggs says: "As the divorce rate in the United States climbs to nearly 50 percent, fathers seem to be disappearing from their daughters' lives. Research shows that girls and young women who have an unstable father figure are more liable to have unplanned pregnancy, low self-esteem, high school and college drop-out, poverty, divorce and sexually promiscuous behavior."

A Fatherless Daughter is a female who grew up with an absent, unattached or unavailable father. This one key missing element in a girl's life can have real negative consequences on her as she becomes a woman. The impact of an absent, unattached or unavailable father on his adult daughter's life is critical when it comes to her self-image, her relationship with men, her work, her friendships and even her relationship with money.

When a girl's father makes it clear to her that she is loved unconditionally, for whom she is, and that he approves of her, he begins to lay a foundation for her healthy sense of self-worth, self-love, and self-value, that will follow her into adulthood.

If, however, the little girl does not have such a relationship with the father, if she sees rejection or emotional coldness or withdrawal from him; if he simply is not available and doesn't provide for her needs, her sense of self-worth will be tainted, her self-confidence warped or non-existent. In addition, her portrait of a loving relationship or her image of provisions may become distorted or dysfunctional, and she may find herself – lacking and feeling unsafe and insecure.

There are four primary basic essentials a young girl needs from her father. She needs his Provision, Protection, Presence and Praise. If these four essential needs are NOT met early on in a girl's life, once she becomes an adult, she begins to feel unsafe, insecure, unwanted, unloved and rejected. There begins the "Making of a Fatherless Daughter Woman.

Studies Show That Females Who Grow Up Fatherless Are:

1. Eight times more likely to go to prison.
2. Five times more likely to commit suicide.
3. Twenty times more likely to have behavioral problems.
4. 32 times more likely to run away.

5   Ten times more likely to abuse chemical substances.
6   Nine times more likely to drop out of high schools
7   33 times more likely to be seriously abused.
8   73 times more likely to be fatally abused.
9   One-tenth as likely to get A's in school.
10 On average have a 44% higher mortality rate.
11 On average have a 72% lower standard of living

The above facts are taken from: US Department Health and Human Services, US Department of Health & Census, Rainbow of All God's Children, Parents of Prison Policy Review 2003 and US Department of Justice Special Report.

Many of the symptoms and patterns found in fatherless daughters are, rage and anger, feelings of abandonment, trust and commitment issues and low self-image. Other symptoms are challenges with shame, sex and intimacy, difficulty in sustaining healthy lasting relationships, driven by success, and issues around money.

The questions that plague many girls and women who are fatherless can be painful.

Our Invisible Cries In The Dark

Several of the questions can look like these:

How could a father abandon his own daughter?

Why is it so hard for you to be a good father to me?

As a father, don't you realize that I need you to make it through life?

As a father, where is your decency?

And the worst one…Daddy, don't you love me?

"Daddy don't you love me?" is a recurring question in the mind of every fatherless daughter. These questions may never get answered, nevertheless, they still needed to be asked. Many of these questions you will read in the letters written in this book.

It was a summer Saturday when approximately sixty five girls, ages 12-17, gathered for The 2015 Fatherless Girls Summit in Columbia, SC. The young girls attended this event to learn how to deal with their pain of fatherlessness. Through a combination of dynamic speakers, music, dance, food and fun, the girls learned valuable lessons on love, acceptance and forgiveness.

One of the sessions included writing a letter to their fathers. They didn't have to worry about being judged, being punished or having anything to prove. They were instructed to write from their hearts. And that's exactly what they did.

As a fatherless girl or woman who read through the letters in this book, it is my hope that you will begin to understand that you are not alone. That there are many girls and women who have traveled this same path. Of course you are wounded, we all have been. Perhaps by someone who no doubt was also wounded. It's not our fault, it's our injury. Yet, you do yourself and the world no good by remaining injured. God put you here on this planet because you are needed and gave you this body, this name, this personality to bring light into the world. And apparently what you can contribute to the world is essential or you wouldn't be here.

To the fathers who will read this book, it is my hope that you will begin to understand the importance of your role in your daughter's life and the pain they carry when daddy isn't there. This book is not about judgment. It's about bringing you awareness to this incredible massive epidemic that's creating so much havoc in the lives of the women and girls affected by it. Therefore, I asked that you don't judge yourself, but allow this awareness to open opportunities for new choices.

I also believe this book will serve as a conversation starter. A dialogue that's long overdue. A conversation that includes everyone, mom, dad and daughter. We will never solve these problems without including everyone. Yet, we must not forget who are the real stars in this story, the leading ladies of the stories…they are the daughters.

This book serves as their voice. The letters are from their hearts of fatherless daughters. We did not edit, tamper or change any of the letters. They are printed in this book exactly as they were written. Read them with some understanding. Read them with compassion. But more importantly, read what is being said with your heart.

Chapter Two

Letters To Daddy

It was a beautiful summer Saturday in June, where 65 girls, ages 12-17, gathered for The 2015 Fatherless Girls Summit in Columbia, SC. They all had something in common. They were fatherless daughters because they each were the product of an unattached, unavailable or absent father. They all carried an emptiness and pain that they found difficult to articulate.

So for six hours incredible speakers, leaders and dance instructors and a powerful DJ helped them to redefine who they were, reclaim their worth and rewrite a new narrative for their lives. They laughed, they danced, they ate, they made new friends, took pictures, shared from their hearts and they cried.

They cried because they wanted what every fatherless girl and woman wants: to be loved and validated by their daddy.

Then it happened. We asked them this question, "If you could say anything to your daddy without getting trouble, without being judged or without being afraid, what would you say?" Many of the girls became emotional because for the first time they were beginning to connect with their hidden pain. One way of releasing the pain is to write it out. That's exactly what they did.

For many, their letters were very short because this was the first time they had a chance to have their voices heard. Several were afraid, but they did it anyway. There were some who were so detached from their pain until they simply couldn't.

Volunteers served as a comfortable arm for many who simply needed to just cry it out. Others wanted to talk it out. Then our special dance leader helped them to dance it out and release. We also prayed and the peace began to settle in the room.

The girls began to write and we felt the fear and the pain lift. We listened as they began to share about the shift they felt within. Many of them understood that their lives would never be the same once they walked out the door. Others shared about the power of forgiveness and how their future now seemed brighter.

As you read these letters, you will find a common thread among them and that's the love they all share for their dad. It's amazing how young people have the ability to love when there seems to be no love directed back to them. You will discover in the letters that many of the girls simply wanted their father's time and presence, not his money.

And while I believe provision is one of the things fathers must provide, at a certain age a daughter simply wants her daddy's presence. I believe as fathers read these letters, they will be challenged and moved into action. By action, I mean truly making an effort to connect and bond with their daughters in a new and fresh way.

It is also my hope that fatherless daughters read these letters and make a quality decision to take the journey of love, acceptance and forgiveness in order to start their healing process.

Our Invisible Cries In The Dark

I would like to take a moment to address the mothers of fatherless daughters who will read these letters. I want to offer you this opportunity to forgive your daughter's father. I encourage you to become the catalyst to helping your daughter and her father's relationship begin to heal. Mothers, you will play an important role in the reunion of the absent father and his daughter to take place.

Often times, mothers hold their own set of wounds. There may be occasions where your own hurt and anger towards your daughter's father will tempt you to try and keep them apart. Please note that I am not talking about those cases where dad is not safe for your daughter to be around. I would never advocate such case.

I am speaking of when you allow your own set of unresolved issues that stems from the relationship or marriage that didn't work out between the two of you get in the way of you allowing dad to see his daughter. There are many cases such as this and it is not in the best interest of the daughter. I say no more to this behavior that no longer serves anyone. Especially your daughter.

If you truly want reconciliation between your daughter and her father, there has to be a healing between you and the father as well. I keep telling everyone that the star of this story is and always will be the daughters. What's best for your daughter is a healthy relationship with her mother and her father.

These letters and this book are not meant to blame, shame or point the finger at fathers of any wrong doing. This book is intended to touch the hearts of its readers. To go into the very space where you've not allowed yourself to be touched before. Inside the deepest part of your hearts. The fathers and mothers who read this will respond with a maternal and paternal care that says "we must save our daughters."

The fatherless daughters and women who will read this book will understand that they are not alone. They will also come to know that they can heal their pain of fatherlessness if they so choose. And more importantly, you have a responsibility to heal. This is not a crutch or an excuse to behave in ways that do not serve your best interest. Whatever your father didn't get right, acknowledge it, forgive and accept what has happened. But know that you and only you get to choose if you will allow what has happened to prevent you from living the life God has created you to live. You deserve to live your truth. You deserve to live your dreams. And if daddy never gets it right, it may be painful, but know that pain can be healed. You are a beautiful divine masterpiece. That's who you are.

Our Invisible Cries In The Dark

In this moment, I release the muted voices of fatherless daughters everywhere. In this moment, your voice is no longer invisible. Your voice is no longer unheard cries. This book serves as the power of a collective voice. The voices of our daughters.

******

Dear Daddy,

I love you so much. I want you to be there for me all the time. My heart has healed at this program I went to called The Fatherless Girls Summit. I've healed for when you and mommy divorced and it made my heart die. This is why I don't listen and I lie. I know you have a job to do, but what's more important, me or your job? I love you and I know you love me. And I know I would never tell this to your face up front. But I want you here with me, my family, your side of the family, our family. From your daughter. **(12 yrs.)**

******

Angela Carr Patterson

Dear Daddy,

I'm not sure what exactly to say, but I'm going to start with, I forgive you for not coming when you said you were. I forgive you for thinking that somehow your money could make everything okay. To be completely honest, I've sort of lost faith in you. I'm 17 now and I don't really know anything about you or my family on your side. But because of today, it's okay. We all go through some things. It's just life.

Yes, you may buy me things and give me money, but that will never amount to the time you didn't spend with me. I don't want the Jordan's or the name brand clothing. I could really care less about them. What I wanted was for you to come when you said you were.

When I got dressed and waited for hours on end, even falling asleep on the couch. You complain to my mom about how you feel you don't know me, but you don't try. When I call, you don't pick up. I really did get the point when I just knew you weren't coming.

And we'll, it hurts, but I forgive you. Because I know without forgiving you, I wouldn't be able to be the best that I can be. Regardless of all the times you let me down, didn't show up to school functions, I still love you because love is the way.

I'm gonna be able to get through this. I was angry. I remember days when I would just sit home in my room and cry because I felt like you didn't love me. I felt like you didn't care about me. I wasn't important. I felt like I wasn't good enough for your time. I was like some charity or some non-profit organization that you send money and clothes to and leave. I've felt inferior and done things I really regret all because I've felt not important to you. I love and forgive you. **(17yrs)**

******

Dear Daddy,

Even though you not there with me every day, I still see you. I know that you care and love me because you show and tell me. I just think that when you were on the streets you could have thought about me and stopped. I get jealous when I see other girls and their dads because I want what they have. I want you to come see me doing things. I want you to take me places. But I know you were young and everyone makes mistakes. But be mindful and think about how it will affect me, your daughter. Whatever happened, I can't change it. I still love you and will always love you because you are my dad. **(13yrs)**

******

Dear Daddy,

I want to first start off by saying, I love you. I love you but there are a few things you do I don't think you understand the effects on me. We live together, you, my mom and I and things aren't great. Out of five girls, with me being the baby and the only child you're raised I know it can be difficult. But I know I also deserve better. I don't know your story and why things are the way they are now but I want to be able to move pass it.

One thing that you could improve on is showing me that I am important. When I try to have conversation, don't make faces as if what I am saying I not important. I never feel comfortable talking to you knowing what I say isn't important and what I say matters.

Spend time with me. Half the time, no the majority of the time, you're on the phone or outside with your friends. If I ask for a hug, you make faces as if it's the worst thing in the world. I know you and my mom aren't happy together.

I know you think staying together until I graduate is the best thing. I honestly just want both of you happy and want to be happy. I want to know you love and care about me. I don't want to be just some mistake.

Maybe you just don't know how to express your feelings, but I'm tired of feeling like the outsider and not having the same relationship with my dad my older sister. Regardless of all we are going through, I still love you and I forgive you for all the hurt and I apologize if I've ever done anything to make you distant. Xoxo, your daughter **(16 yrs.)**

******

Dear Daddy,

You probably haven't been in my life and my mom has pushed you away. I still love you. But, I wish you were here with me because all of my other friends have two people to come to. Why don't you want to be in my life?

I know you got other children. Out of all of them, why couldn't you be there mentally? My mom not always there for me. I just want a father figure in my life. I don't always need money. I need advice or someone just to lean on when I am sad. You could tell me right from wrong.

My friends always says their dad is their first love. My first love is a hard headed boy. Why it couldn't be you as my first love? I just need someone to lean on. Dad, I love you. I just wish you were here. I am tired of all these men pretending to be my dad. Why couldn't you be here? **(15 yr.)**

******

Dear Daddy,

I just wanted you to know that I forgive you for not being there at my graduation. I also forgive you for not doing anything. Really, I sort of realized that if you're not around I will have to fight and protect myself and not let you being away or anything break me down.

Really, I just wanted you to be there when I turned 10. Now I am 13. A girl needs her dad during her teenage years or at least you could have said, hi, without me having to talk to you first. I was mad at you for not reading or even responding to my letter.

But I forgive you for that and maybe I can get pass you not being there. You wasn't there when I needed you, but it's cool. You were busy and I forgive you for not being there during my 8th grade promotions. When I got a principal's award, I just wanted to say thanks for not being there. Now, I am must stronger. **(13 yrs)**

******

Dear Daddy,

The last time we saw each other you acted as if you never knew me. You acted as if I wasn't your daughter. You acted as if you didn't want to be bothered with me.

Even though you lived in the house with me and my mom for 14 years. For those 14 years of my life, you were always unattached. I mean when I was little we were close but then you began to distance yourself. My mother always provided and was always attentive to me when you were there and when you weren't.

The moment you chose to hurt my mother, I didn't know why and to this day, I still can't understand why you chose another woman over my mom. I don't know how long it may take for me to fully forgive you, but I am going to try to make sure that I live my life without holding grudges again you for not being there.

You're my father but in my mind you're on my dad or someone who was in the house with me. You may care and love me but you don't know how to show it. One day I hope you'll come around. Love, your daughter **(15yrs.)**

******

Dear Daddy,

Growing up, the feeling you gave me was beyond amazing. The love you showed, as well as the attention was great. Until the unexpected that I prayed would never happen…happened.

Ever since you've left, my heart has broken. Especially to hear you had moved on with another lady. Now, you're showing me half of the attention I'm used to. It seems like you never have time for me anymore. You put her before me. You affected me the most because of the fact that I was daddy's little girl, and you only talk to me when you feel like it.

I go anywhere to get attention. Even though you buy me anything I want, the love, laughter and attention is what I miss. Ever since, my worth is questioned.

I wonder everyday how much I mean to boys, as well as others. Am I enough? Will you leave me? Can you stay around?

I feel also, as if I am in competition with every other female. The same way I feel as I compete with your girlfriend. Life goes on though. It's not stopping me from my success. **(17yrs)**

******

Dear Daddy,

You promised me things that you knew yourself you weren't going to do. You said, "I love you," but the thing is, did you really mean it? Because it is one thing for someone to tell you something and mean it, but if you say it and don't mean it, it's hard to trust you.

When I get older and start dating, you know what guys are going to say? I have trust issues and it comes from you. Parents usually apologize when they are wrong but It is so crazy how all you do is hurt me and apologize.

You are my father and I love you to death, but you know it's sad how when my mother even talks to a guy, I get angry because of you and no one should be like that. To be honest, I could sit back and laugh because you always tell me that you wish you could've done better, but you still haven't tried.

It's okay because I am an empowered young woman and I can't let you hurt me anymore. Tears were shed but they are gone. Now I just hope that when I get older and have kids that you will do better and turn your story around. **(13 yrs)**

******

Dear Daddy,

Hey dad it has been a long time since we talked. I want you to know I love you. All I want is for you to be in my life when I am hurting. Okay, so the last time we talked was January and I was in a restaurant.

So many times I don't feel like you care and I feel like I need a boy to love me. And yeah, I know I don't need that …all I need is you.

How do you feel about me? Did I do something wrong? I really love you. Do you love me? God brought you into this world for many reasons and one of them is to love me and other people you really care about. I had to learn that from my mom. Come on, I know you can do it. (**13 yrs**)

Our Invisible Cries In The Dark

******

Dear Daddy,

I want you to know that I am releasing. Dad, I am done crying and staying up wondering if you care or not. I am not sure if you care and honestly, it's okay. I am getting stronger and walking like a champion.

You were there. You never showed me what it was like to be a daddy's little girl. You probably didn't have a good of life and tried to do your best. But it wasn't good enough.

I just hope you have a good life, living it up with your new wife and kids. I won't know what it is like to have you brag on me I can truly say I am happy you aren't here. This is God telling me what to avoid.

Money doesn't cover your invisibility from my life. You may not ever reach out to me again and that' okay. I forgive you. This journey for me is just starting and the plan God has for me is so great. I can feel it now. I just know in here. Life is going to happen, but I will be strong. I know it is going to take time but in the end, it will be all worth it.

Like one of favorite songs said, "I'm the fatherless, they find their rest at the sound of your Great name." I have found my rest and I plan on keeping it. How about you? **(15 yrs)**

******

Dear Daddy,

You might now know this but you really did hurt me. I wish you happiness even though you might not ever care. Wiz Khalifa once told me to "never cry over something more than once," So after me crying for you one time too many, I vowed to myself I would never cry over you again.

I don't know how you could just up and leave knowing I would need you one day. You left, why? I will never know the real reason. You were supposed to show me how to be loved and how to value love. I hate you but that is a strong word. I can't say that I love you because that would be too strong of a word as well.

Cry over somebody that's supposed to be in my life…no I don't think so. Life goes on and I will move on too. I'll be successful without you. I'll have the nicest things, I'll have kids and make sure they have a better life than I ever had because there's nothing you could teach me. How could you couldn't stay? **(13yrs)**

******

Our Invisible Cries In The Dark

Dear Daddy,

I remember being little about 3 or 4 years old. I remember being with you and after leaving I cried every time.

Then it started to change. You didn't pick up any more after a while. You didn't come see me for my birthday anymore. I began to get sad because at that age or 6, 7, 8 and under you meant the world to me.

After all those years, leaving to stay with you during the summer break at age 11 or 12 was hard. I always questioned if you cared and did why didn't you try harder? Being with out you almost every day makes me feel angry, alone and depressed and not cared about.

I also always think I'm just the child out of all of my siblings whose dad is just not here for me. I know that you buy me things but sometimes it should be a little more than that.

You have other kids and my mama has me and other kids. But the kids you are with and the kids that my mama has except me have a dad that calls or spend time with them. When I think about that all I think of is only having a mom. It make me feel alone.

I am gonna end with the last time you made me upset. It was when you texted, not call, and asked when I get out of school. I told you that we were already out and that I was free that week. You didn't ever respond. It made me feel like you didn't care. And I just wanted to give up on trying to spend time with you. **(15 yrs)**

******

Dear Daddy,

I really want us to spend more time together. I know when I go to my grandma, I spend more time with her than I do with you. I felt like you just didn't want to spend with me. I would try and make you laugh or start a conversation with you, but you always on your phone.

Dad I was really mad when you didn't come to my 5th grade graduation. I really wanted you to see me walk across the stage. I will graduate in 4 more years. Will you see me walk across the stage? Will you be there for me?

When you dated your girlfriend, I felt like you paid her more attention than you did me. She would look at me any kind of way and she way stuff about me (that's what I felt). Didn't like her at all.

Before I really wanted you and my mom to get back together. But now she is happy and that's all I really wanted for her. I love you so much daddy and I am not mad no more. Because I let go of the hurt and the pain because I love you. **(14 yrs)**

******

Dear Daddy,

You have made a huge impact on my life. Both positive and negative. You gave me everything I needed and was very close with me the first six years of my life. And then you started to separate every year after that.

You were still in my and my brother's lives, but it wasn't like those other six years. When I got in teenage years, I started misbehaving and doing things that were not right. I wanted to do things I enjoyed and I couldn't because mama was all by herself. She had to choose between my activities I liked or my brother's activities.

It was plenty of times that I cried and said that I wanted to come live with you to be able to do those things. I've even called crying to you telling you all the things I've been missing out on. You said it would get better soon and that you were working on a plan to give me everything that would make me happy. Thank you for believing in me and trying to do better in my life. **(13 yrs)**

******

Dear Daddy,

Honestly daddy I love you. For the longest time I was a daddy's girl. Even when you weren't home (which was a lot), I loved you. I had dreams of you walking me down the aisle even though you never have and still don't approve of me talking to boys.

There were many times when I felt that you treated my other sister better than me. Even though you always called me us your little girls.

Eventually thought the years I felt isolated. You had a relationship and lived with my oldest sister as well as my two younger sisters. But never once have you lived with me for more than a couple of months. You've been in and out of jail dealing with your baby mama. I don't live with my birth mom but I know she will never put you in jail. Yet, still you ran to these women.

I remember one time you got out of jail and we were on the phone and you promised me that you would never go to jail again. And I believed you. I remember after that, a couple of months later, trying to call you for close to a week or two. You wouldn't pick up the phone. I kept asking my mama (biologically my grandmother) why you weren't picking up the phone? And one day this call comes in and ask would I like to accept this call and it was you daddy.

You lied to me. You told me that you would not go back to jail. Yet, now you are sitting and calling me from jail. How can you promise your daughter that you're not going to do something, yet you go and do the exact thing you promised not to do? That's the first time I've ever said, maybe I am not a daddy's girl. The first time I ever didn't trust my father. The first time I ever said, okay do what you want, I don't care. And then from that point on I took what you said with a couple grains of salt.

If you said you was coming home, I would say I'll see if you come home. And then in 2013 I believed that was a moment when I labeled you a sperm donor because you did something to me that literally killed me inside and because of that I potentially may not have been here. You put me in a deep depressed state.

I'm going to explain. I hadn't seen you in I think a year or more. And when you walked in the house, I tried to get a hug and you looked me almost like I was crazy. Your mother actually said, your daughter wants a hug. **(17yrs)**

******

Dear Daddy,

I want you to know that even though you haven't been around as much, I still love you. It just hurts me that you don't call to check up on me or come to see me. I would love to see you and spend time with you because I love you. What I don't understand is why you don't call or come to see me? Don't you love me? That I a question I always ask. I know you say it, but do you mean it? **(12yrs)**

******

Dear Daddy,

Why would you abandon your own child? I know you been through a lot when you were younger. But with you having your own child, you could have at least changed that.

A daughter needs love and needs to hear her father say, I love you, you're beautiful and I will never leave you. I love you daddy, but there are a lot of things you need to change.

Because it's not fair that you show a child that isn't yours and two kids that are more love than you've ever shown me. But I will be fine because after seven years, I finally found and worked up enough courage to forgive you. For that I feel better.

I learned that I can't change you, you have to work up the courage to do this on your own. I was hurting for a long time, then you reached out two years ago making promises getting me happy, then you forgot about the promises. You always make me think it was my fault, but I know it's not. I love you daddy and I pray that you change. **(14 yrs)**

******

Dear Daddy,

Why would you leave me behind? I remember you coming around when I was little. Now you don't. You hurt me and my mom very bad.

I have a father figure in my life and he is doing a damn good job and better job than you. You don't want to hear from me or my mom but at least I am making an effort. You aren't. You are stupid for what you did.

My mom is happily married to a wonderful man. She is happy and pregnant and things are going good. I am hurt because you never come around and it isn't fair and if you think it's too late to come in my life, well you are wrong. I need my dad. You must be selfish to leave me and my sister and get married and have more kids. I love you but you hurt me. **(13yrs)**

******

Dear Daddy,

I grew up with you around but that eventually went away and you were barely there. It went from you calling every day to hearing from you every few months. You were somewhat there but that's not what I wanted.

I could care less about material things; I just wanted to know you were there supportively and cared. You not being there took a toll on me. I started to push people away, held built up anger that wasn't healthy.

I would cry myself to sleep at night wondering why you didn't love me or if you did why don't you show it. I wanted all the pain to go away and not have to deal with and actually thought about killing myself.

I know I have a purpose in life and dreams/goals that I want to accomplish so I pushed myself forward and try to think positive. To do that I have to forgive you and release all the anger I have. Not for you but for me and I do. I forgive you. **(15 yr)**

******

"24 million children live in biological father-absent homes.1 in 3 American children grow up without a father."— -US Census Bureau

Dear Daddy,

I would wish for time to start over. I wish you didn't hurt mommy. You made a big change on my life. For example, relationships, family, trust. It kills me that I had to go through this, but I do. I say mean things to you that I don't mean, but hopefully I'll get over it and attempt to talk to you. I know that going to be hard. But I can say that at times I do miss your presence, but I will never get over what you did to me and my mommy. Mostly the family we were supposed to have. But I do wish you the best. **(14yrs)**

******

Dear Daddy,

I wish you were more active in my life. Even if it were just calling more often, do something. I need a father in my life. Yes, I do have father figures in my life. Many of them, but it not the same as having an actual father with me. And even if you don't hear it as often as you could, just know that I love you. **(13yrs)**

******

Dear Daddy,

All I have to say is that I wish you were in my life. I know it may seem like you're there, but it's the things that you have to do to be there. Just because you and my mom break up doesn't mean you have to break up with me.

But I forgive you and if I don't this will be haunting me for the rest of my life. I wish that you would get your life together and I don't wish nothing bad on you. You need to change so that you can really be in my life. That's all I got to say about that. **(12 yrs)**

******

Dear Daddy,

I am wanting for you to try and help us out more. What I mean is I want you to try and come see us as much as possible because we can't come to you all the time. I would like for you to try and see if you can work something out where y'all live in the same household so I can see you and not just hear over the phone how much you love me. I just want to hear it face to face. I also want to say thank you for not leaving me and my brother. I appreciate you being there whenever you can. **(13 yrs)**

******

Dear Daddy,

I know you have seven kids but you only take took care of one. What about your other six kids? You wonder why when you come around we act like how we act. We never see you.

Me and you have the same birthday and you never told me happy birthday. You came to my other siblings' graduation, but never once came to anything else. You owe us a lot. I really don't' want you in my life.

I've gotten older now and I'm over it. No need to stress over you. I really needed you at time, but it's too late now to be honest. I forgive you for everything but I'll never forget. **(15yrs)**

******

Dear Daddy,

I thank you for surprising me so much and blessing me. You gave me a good girl thing and you bring my heart so much. I want you to know I love you so much and blessing me daddy, I love you. You have done so much for me and helped me in my 10 years of life. Dad I love you. You have put a beautiful life in me. You brighten my day. You always been there for me ever since I was a little girl. Thank you for supporting me. **(10 yrs)**

*****

Dear Daddy,

You have been there for me since birth and you have never let me down and you have been in jail and out but that never stopped you from caring and loving me.

But now you have went back to jail even though you promised you wouldn't go back to jail. Even though you promised you wouldn't go back.

Know it's like I am invisible. You haven't called me since you went jail and I call my aunts and they say you have money to make phone calls. But if that's true why don't you call me or send me money. I worry sometimes and this is the first summer I am spending without you. When will you call me? Hopefully before my birthday. **(13 yrs)**

******

Dear Daddy,

Our Invisible Cries In The Dark

How are you doing? I miss you. I hope you are doing well. Because I am. I think about you every day. Sometimes I cry and I wonder where are you?

I love you daddy. I would like to get together with my brothers and sisters that I have. But I do know that I have two little brothers. I would like to see them and you again.

By the way, my uncle that was like a dad to me, passed away. He might be gone, but never forgotten. And the same for you, daddy. You will never be forgotten. I love you and miss you dearly. I would like to meet with you again soon. **(13 yrs)**

******

"The ache for a father's love is a temporary description. Not a permanent definition of our souls."—**Kia Stephens**

Dear Daddy,

I love you to the moon and back. I forgive you for all the times I didn't agree with what you did. Even though we not in contact much, I hope I still mean something to you. **(12 yrs)**

******

Dear Daddy,

I miss you. Your personality. How you always have a positive attitude. How you always keep smile on your face. How you never gave up. **12 yrs**

******

Dear Daddy,

I hope you are doing well. I am. I mean, I really miss you and wished you loved me, like I love you. I understand sometimes life is hard. I am doing good, but it's not the same without having you around. I don't feel like I have a dad anymore. Please show me you still care. (**14yrs**)

******

Now it's your turn. What would you say to your father if you had nothing to fear, or nothing to prove? I want you take a moment and think about all the feelings inside of you. What is it that you want your father to know? If you are a fatherless girl, I want you to begin writing now. (Fatherless Women, you will have a chance to write your letter in a later chapter). Don't stop writing until you have said everything you've ever wanted to say. Once you are done, take a deep breath and say a prayer. It is entirely up to you if you want to give the letter to your dad or not. Because what's important is that you've found the courage to speak your **truth.**

Our Invisible Cries In The Dark

Dear Daddy,

Angela Carr Patterson

Chapter Three

Fatherless Women Un-Mute

It doesn't matter how old you are, the pain of fatherlessness still hurts. I work with women from around the world who continue to struggle with not having their father's love. I remember having a phone conversation with a woman who was 81 years old. She was crying profusely because her father rejected her when she was six years old. He told a group of people that she was not his daughter. She carried that pain inside for seventy five years. Her pain was just as raw at eighty one as it was at age six. Throughout her adult life she experienced a lot of illness and sickness in her body. I truly believe the pain that she carried manifested in her body.

There are millions of women with unresolved daddy issues. These issues are playing out in their lives at home, in their marriages, the workplace, in their bank accounts and their bodies. Through my programs and services, we have seen many of these women heal their daddy wounds and rewrite a new story in their lives.

Yet, there are countless women who are not even aware that the fatherless daughter syndrome is playing out in their lives. They experience issues in their relationships and somehow find a way to blame the other person. If the truth were told, these patterns recycle when they move on to new relationships.

For me, I simply thought my issues were a personal failure on my part. I didn't have a clue that my inabilities to sustain healthy relationships, or be successful in my career or lack of self-confidence were all stemming from having an absent father in my life.

But as I began to dig deeper, I discovered some real truths. I've since healed many of my daddy wounds. I wish I could say that my triggers no longer surface. Because sometimes they do. And when they do, I simply shift and remember who I am beyond my fatherlessness.

Our Invisible Cries In The Dark

In this chapter, we are going to share some letters from women who grew up as fatherless daughters. The ages range from age twenty seven to seventy seven. You will notice that these letters are much longer than those of the younger girls. That's because the years of pain and wounds are longer. Many of these women are very educated, professional and successful women. Yet they still long for daddy's love and acceptance.

Whether we are fifteen or fifty, we still long to be loved and validated by our fathers.

******

Dear Dad???,

I really didn't question why you were not in my life, because when I got old enough my mother told us why you were not around. My Mom did everything for us. She taught us right from wrong and instilled great morals and values. When I was old enough to learn that your mother and father, my grandma and grandpa lived just around the corner from us, I wanted to meet them.

I met them alone with my aunts, uncles and cousins and they all said we looked just like you and your other children. At that time I had never seen your other children, but I knew that you were with them and not us. As my mother raised us, I wondered why was she so strict and always would explain how disappointed she would be if we did something wrong. Mom would ask neighbors to look after us, and if we did anything wrong they had permission to spank us.

Mom never talked bad about you and we never wanted for anything. So I thought it was ok not to have a dad in the house because everything was good without you. When my mom married our step-father, he gave us everything we wanted. And what we wanted was to have him around, but he worked very long hours. As time went on he was our father and I or my brother and sister never asked for you. You never came around or brought gifts to us.

Now that I am older, I often think about why you never tried to have a relationship with us? Why you loved your other kids and not us? What did my mom do wrong? Why is it that your other children are all so bad?

Dad, I just wanted to tell you that you missed out on some GREAT SUCCESSFUL KIDS! We are all doing our thing and loving our children, even though I don't have any children. All I can say is thank you for giving me life.

******

Our Invisible Cries In The Dark

Dear Daddy,

You left me. You wouldn't help me when I asked you for college. You told me no. I didn't know how to love or how to receive love from men. I always thought that I had to do everything by myself. That no man would ever amount to anything. You moved on with your life, started a new family and never looked back...maybe once or twice. I really though we have bond, but we didn't. I have memories of you being a great dad. Fun times, good food going to the candy store, etc. but when I needed you the most you were nowhere to be found. I lost my mind and gave away my body searching for your love. Never found it.

Today, I am married. I have a daughter who I though was going to grow up fatherless, like me. I had to learn to pray and forgive because I blamed you for not teaching me how to keep a man. So much surfaces from being fatherless. I almost missed my mark. But God. He healed and restored every broken piece made me new. Twenty seven years old entrepreneur, wife, mother of one and one on the way. Sorry you chose not to be a part of my life. No hard feelings. I love you just the same.

******

Angela Carr Patterson

Dear Dad,

As a young girl, when my mom asked me how I was feeling about you not being there, I used to say, "how can I miss what I never had?" The truth is that I was sad, angry, and confused about you not filling an active role as my father. It wasn't until my early adult life that I was able to understand and admit that I was actually deeply impacted by your absence and had been journeying through life with a broken heart. A piece of me was missing because you weren't there. I had so many questions that begged for answers. Why couldn't you just do what you said you were going to do? Why was it so hard for you to love me? What father wouldn't want to do everything he could for his daughter? Was I lovable? Could I ever be "ok"? Did you know that I needed you?

I know you think I "turned out fine" because I have several degrees and have always pursued my dreams, but I struggle too. I've needed your protection, affirmation, blessing, and presence. I wish you had been there to show me what it means to be loved, cherished, respected and cared for by a man. Even now as an adult woman, I deal with wondering how different my life would have and could have been if I had a strong and loving man as my father here on earth. What would it be like to be "daddy's little girl" and to rest in the loving and secure embrace of a daddy? You are so far away physically, emotionally, and spiritually.

I can pick up the phone and talk to you right now, but Schizophrenia and drug abuse took you away from me a long time ago. I used to think it was a choice you made intentionally not to be around and now I can see that there is more to the story. This has not made it any less difficult to be a fatherless daughter. Although you as my biological father cannot be here for me, I have to remind myself daily that God is my father and that He loves me. I have determined to forgive you every time I am reminded of this "daddy wound," and I do forgive you. The truth is that there will always be a place for you in my heart.

******

Dear Daddy,

I even feel funny typing the word daddy because I've never had the pleasure of saying that to anyone. Especially you, because you were never around for me to call you daddy. I can remember as a little girl longing for you. Wondering why I never heard from you? Why you never called? Was I even a thought in your mind?

I remember making up stories in my mind that one day you would drive up to our house and I would run to you and be swept up in your arms. You would squeeze me tight and say "Hi daddy's girl."

You will never know how I longed for that day to be called "daddy's little princess." Yet, it never happened. You never came for me. So, when I got older, I came for you. I remember the first drive to visit you. I was married and had one child. It was the longest drive of my life because I didn't know what to expect. When I laid eyes on you, I could see so much of me in your physical presence. Yet, there was no real connection.

You seemed happy to see me. I must admit, I was scared. I didn't know you. I knew you were my father and I knew I was suppose to love you. But it didn't feel like love. It felt more like I was meeting a stranger. You were a stranger and you were my dad.

Over the years, we talked on the phone. Never anything deep and never over 3-5 minutes at a time. You called to say hello and that you were doing well. You asked how I was doing and that was it.

Somewhere deep within me I knew that you loved me. I also knew that you had so many issues that prevented you from demonstrating that love. I would find myself angry because I wanted to know why you never came to see me when you were well? Why did I have to meet you when you were ill. I never had at the opportunity of having a relationship with that dad.

I felt robbed and cheated. You did that to me. I tried to let you off the hook because of your illness, but the truth is, you were not always sick. I just was never a priority. I finally accepted that truth. All I wanted from you was you.

I would write you letters as a young girl and run to the mail box hoping you would write back. You never wrote one word on the paper that you wrapped the money inside. Did you not have anything to say to me? Could you not even muster up a "Hello?"

I never could understand that. You would send money inside of a blank sheet of paper and not even share a sentence with me. I didn't want or need your money. Mom had it all under control. I grew up with everything girl could ever want…except her dad's love and validation.

This missing link caused a lot of self rejection and low self esteem. I never felt good enough. It showed up in my marriage, my friendships and even in my ability to raise my children effectively. Little did I know that I was angry. Seething angry and in many ways I took it out on them.

I felt damaged. I felt ashamed. I felt unlovable. All of these feelings hindered me and prevented me from living full out.

I remember receiving the call that you were dying. As I arrived at the hospital, they said you hadn't eaten in a few days. I was able to get you to eat. I remember feeding you and thinking to myself, "I'm doing for you what you never did for me." In that moment, I felt an overwhelming amount of love and compassion for you. You realized it was me and you sat up and began to talk and laugh. You were happy to see me. It was the first time I'd ever enjoyed my time with you. I felt special because I was the only one who could get you to eat. I loved you in that moment. Truly loved you and for the first time I felt a connection to you. My daughter video taped it. It's the only picture I have of you and I together.

I left that hospital free. My next visit you were in hospice and they had given you something for the pain. You were asleep. I simply set there for 2 hours and watched you sleep. I met your doctors. No one knew about me. They didn't know that I existed. By that time, I was so use to not being identified as your daughter that it didn't matter. I wanted the time together with you to be one of love, peace and forgiveness. It was.

A week later, I received a call from the hospital that you had died. I screamed. And immediately I wondered why? Why did I scream? Was I hurt that you were gone? Or was I hurt because the finality of never ever having what I wanted from you? To be the twinkle in your eyes. To feel your love. I don't know. I was just hurt.

As I attended your funeral, I sat in the back of church. I am your only child and I was sitting in the back of the church at your funereal. I felt like a stranger as I watched your family members walk in and many who looked just like me. A man who looked like you was doing the eulogy.

I just assumed he was your brother and my uncle. And he was.

At the burial I was asked to sit with the family. I sat near your brother and my cousin. It was a military service and as they folded the flag, they handed it to my cousin. He refused and pointed towards me. They handed it to my uncle. He refused and pointed to me. They handed it to me and said some words. I don't remember what was said because that's when the floodgates of emotions began. I cried. I cried because I will never ever experience your love the way I needed it. I cried because at last, I was finally validated as your daughter. I cried because I knew this was closure for me.

What I know for sure is that when you and my mom married, you loved each other. I was conceived in love. While you never knew how to demonstrate it to me, you did what you knew. I have forgiven you. And while our phone calls never lasted more than five minutes, you would always end them with "I love you baby" I can hear those words now. I hold those words in my heart. Because that's as close as I will ever get to being "Daddy's little girl." And in some odd way, that really is enough now. I love you daddy and RIP.

Our Invisible Cries In The Dark

******

Letter to my father:

I look around and see the father's involvement in their daughters lives and wonder why I couldn't have had that too. I grew up envying my friends' relationship with their fathers because I didn't have that. I remember growing up wanting to leave home, like my sisters did. Like the time we actually moved out and in with a family friend. I didn't want to move back in but of course we did. Mom thought things would change for the better, but even at that age I knew they wouldn't. All was good for a while until it wasn't. The night before I left for the Army, you and Mom were in the basement fighting, and you were breaking her mother's dishes. What a send off!! Most of my memories are of you and mom fighting, the four of us kids (then two, after my sisters left) being punished for "our crimes", mostly when you were drunk. Yes there were happy times, but those don't always float to the top.

We never had that father daughter relationship that my other friends and classmates had. We never went on daddy-daughter dates, went to dances, etc. We didn't take drives or walks to talk about school, God, growing up, nothing. You either were asleep because you had been drinking or because you had to get up early In the morning. Yes, you provided the basics, food, clothing, shelter, but lacked the tenderness, compassion and emotions. I yearned for that connection with you. I remember how giving and selfless you were to others, your friends, the people at the church, and those at the bar. Your love was conditional, based on if I did my chores, cooked dinner on time, if you were sober. The only times I remember going out as father daughter was after I had left home and joined the service. I would come home on leave and we would go to the bar for lunch or dinner. You seemed proud of me then. I'm sorry that I didn't see or feel that pride from you when I was growing up.

Years later I discovered the secret you had always kept. Years after you were already gone. I began to understand why I joined the Army, to get away from home. It makes sense why I was so vulnerable and naive in the military, looking, searching for approval from those over me. Always trying to fit in, make my superiors proud. The pattern continued in the military with the abuse, but I couldn't say anything, because I wanted to be accepted, to have my father's approval. I did what I thought I should do to get your approval and unconditional love, even years after you were gone. I stayed in the service for 21 years, because I longed for that acceptance.

It wasn't until I allowed Christ into my heart that I began to know what I'd really been searching for my whole life: that unconditional love! Yet the rejection and abandonment I felt from you continued on. I struggled with relationships because I tried too hard to please them. My youngest daughter's father is just like you.... a man who is emotionally and physically unavailable to be a father. Incapable of having and nurturing that relationship with her, teaching her what it's like to be treated by a gentlemen. She's grown up without a father being present in her life. She yearns for that relationship, as I do too. I want so much more for her, much more than I received. I want this cycle to be broken. I want her to know her father and have him experience the beauty of who she is. I want her to have that loving relationship with her uncle, yours own son, but he's emotionally unavailable and keeps himself at a distance.

I'm thankful she and I have a relationship with Christ, because we can experience unconditional love. We've been blessed with men of godly character in our lives.

As for me dad, I'm still single, never been married. I'm still searching for my father's love. I'm still wary of being in a relationship because I'm afraid they wont be emotionally available or that they will abuse me or that they won't love me. I'm still trying to fit in and receive the approval from the men in my life, both professionally and personally. I'm sure you did the best you could with what you knew. You've moved on and we can never have tomorrow, but my daughters can. And this cycle will be broken. Your daughter...

******

Dear Dad,

I am writing this letter because I am finally ready to share my heart with you. When I first sat down to write my mind went blank. I thought: "What would I say? How honest should I be? I stepped away for a minute to collect my thoughts. When I finally sat in from of my computer I decided to share my heart with you. So here it goes!

Did you know that I often thought I was adopted? I used to believe that God made a mistake. How could a loving God give me a father like you? I often asked. Being raised by my grandmother , your mother, during my formative years was the best thing you did for me. At least that is what I thought for many years. Being the oldest daughter, I often felt you were tougher on me than you should have been. Growing up I offered wondered why. You paid more attention to your alcohol, job and TV then you did to me and my sisters – at least that is what I remembered.

I remember how abusive you were to us. I thought that was normal. When you and mom had huge fights you would gather us kids together so we could see and hear you apologizing to each other. You know seeing that made me think that was how love was suppose to be. Every relationship I had was modeled after you. I was searching for my daddy in every guy I dated. They were always way older than me. They said all the right things to make me feel good about myself. I never felt pretty enough. I hated how I looked – big head, big eyes, big lips, nappy hair and a skinny body. You never told me that I was pretty or loved. What made matters worse is that I was told you wanted your first born to be a boy. I can only imagine how you felt when I was your first born. Somehow I tied you giving me to your mother to raise me to you not wanting me. So I always felt like the outsider. I always felt I could never please you no matter what I did. I just felt that I was not good enough to be your daughter.

I longed for my daddy. I just wanted you to be proud of me just because. I needed direction and you were not able to give it to me. I wanted your love and approval and did not get that. I wanted to share my hurts, my victories – I just wanted to share everything with you. I just wanted my daddy. Well that never happened. What I've come to realize is that you just were not able to be there in the way I wanted. It affected me emotionally. It affected my choice in men. It affected how I related to people period. It caused me to pretend that I was adopted. Doing that made it a little easier to live – at least that is what I told myself. The truth is it did not take away the pain. Eventually I found my way. I got a lot of bumps and bruises on the way, yet I made it through.

When you got really sick, I push aside everything I felt to be there for you because you are my dad and I loved you no matter what. You were surprise to see me which told me you did not think I would show up. I had to because you are my dad no matter what. I will always cherish the last letter you wrote to me saying how much you loved me; how very proud of me you were; and asking forgiveness. I waited my whole life to hear that from you. It meant the world to me. When God called you home, I was angry because we were just beginning to heal our relationship and then you were gone. I felt abandoned all over again. Why now? I asked God. It just did not seem fair. I wish we could have a do over and spend more time together. Selah

What I want you to know now is that I carry you in my heart. I have healed my emotional wounds. I married an awesome man of whom you would approve. LOL!!! I am doing well for myself. I think you would be proud of the woman I've become. Dad, I know you did the best you could with what you were taught and shown. I understand that now.

I forgive dad you for everything! All is well with my heart and soul! I will always love you!
Love, Your daughter

******

Dear Daddy,

As I sit here and ponder about what to say, my logic eludes me and I am led to allow the little girl inside to speak to you instead. She has been trapped inside of her own world afraid to come out for fear of what lies on the other side of THAT door. I told her, it was time and there was nothing to be afraid of since I had taken care of the biggest issue we faced...forgiveness of her lost innocence. So the voice you will hear is hers and I free her to speak candidly...

"Why didn't you come for me? Why didn't you visit as grandma told you to? Was I a part of a past you wanted to forget? Was I not pretty enough? Or, did I do something wrong? I remember talking to a man when I was nine and showing him my drawings. I remember that grandma left me alone with you for a long time which was something she never did...so you must have been important. But I never saw you again. After your sister told me about you, and you visited, you didn't come back. I actually didn't hear about you until I was 17 years old. By then, I didn't want to know who you were. I accepted the man I thought was my daddy, although he wanted nothing to do with me either. I had become accustomed to being the "black sheep" and by myself. Thinking back now, this is what has become my reality...

My momma was dead and every father figure in my life wasn't worth me caring about. My step- father, took my innocence from the time I was five until I was almost seven when I told momma, and when she confronted him, and asked for a divorce, he decided that if he couldn't have her, no one would...he made good on his promise when he told me NOT to tell. (I had to live with that. Maybe I shouldn't have told) I cried out in the dark for you every time he hurt me...but you never came. I kept wondering, 'Where was my daddy? Why didn't he make this stop?' So the silence and dark shadows were my comfort and they have been ever since. Grandma later took me and my brother in and the man I was told was my daddy did not want the responsibility, I guess I was damaged goods. Kids picked at me and my brother calling us names because we didn't have a momma or a daddy and so we learned to depend on each other. My friends and cousins came to my games, you weren't there. Father's Day was just another day. While the other children made cards, I drew pictures and colored. The man who took your place never really believed I was his, so there wasn't any effort put forth in being there, and he had more children and since I was labeled a "bastard" child born to a teenage mother, I wasn't a likely choice in the "daddy's little girl" category, his daughter was. She had everything, while I had what my grandmother did her best to provide, but don't worry, I appreciate it now. Besides, God gave me gifts to occupy my time and I buried my time inside my art, my poetry, my school books, and everything that people said I wouldn't be...guess what? I became that and MORE! I made it out of school without any kids and grew up STRONG. Matter of fact, by the time I heard about you again my senior year, you weren't a desire anymore. I told myself, I didn't need a daddy because Jesus was my dad and He did just fine. As time went by, this part of me stayed behind and just decided it was easier not to go any further. The walls I built kept her protected in the world that she had become adjusted to and the stronger side of me took over from there. So see...You don't have to make it up to me, it doesn't matter anyways. I don't care."

Well, that is all she had to say, but I will pick up from where she left off, as usual. When your sister approached me again during her illness when I was 33, I still didn't see the need to know you. My life was already a living hell, except for my kids; men were just a means to an end. I had no example of what a "real" man was, or what I should expect from one except what my grandmother told me and trust me...it was not good. According to her, "If you knew what I knew, you'd leave a man where they at." I did at that point; realize what she meant and why she felt that way. Although I was tricked into meeting you, at first, I was angry...confused and disappointed. I didn't speak to you for six months because I had to figure things out...but eventually realized that my mother wasn't there to defend her reasons, and I had learned why--the hard way. You deserved a chance...at least a chance for me to see the part of me I'd been missing. It's been thirteen years now and we have grown closer, but somehow I still feel a gap in our bond. I have come to love you and I know you love me. You are definitely more loving than the person I took to be my father, which makes me wonder, what type of life I could have had, if you'd been there somehow. I know you can't restore the lost years, however, I had to learn how to turn anger into forgiveness and hate into love. I just want you to know, I forgave my step-father for his murderous act and my innocence stolen, which set me free from THAT bondage. It still hurts, but I don't live in his fearsome shadow any longer. I forgave the man who wasn't there standing in for you...and I don't blame him anymore. I forgive you for not being there, because at least, you have shown me that you did keep up with what I was doing, and you have been there ever since. Even calling me your "Number One". I just wish I could change the way I feel at times. But I know time heals all wounds. You see...I have found a man who is not like the other men in my life. He has accepted me with all of my flaws, past, and even vowed to love me beyond my pain, so I am good. (One less worry for you) And just so you know...I unlocked the door today after writing this letter to the scared little girl inside of me and let her out. The world has changed, but she seemed relieved to be out of...PANDORA'S BOX.

Love,
Finally Daddy's little girl

******

I know that you were indeed moved by such transparency and honesty these women shared. It's not always easy to tell the truth. Especially when the truth is wrapped in so much pain. But the greatest gift that you give yourself is to tell the truth…to yourself first.

Now as a fatherless woman, it's your turn to speak to your father. Even if your dad is no longer alive, this little exercise will help you in ways you've not imagined. If you had nothing to prove, nothing to pretend and nothing to protect, what would you say to your father? Take a moment and write your letter below. As I stated before, it's totally up to you if you want to give the letter to your dad. This is more about you and your freedom than it is about him.

Many of you will be afraid of this task. You may even tell yourself that you will write the letter once you're done reading the book. I want to warn you that it's your fear that's keeping you from writing it now. Fearful of what you may awakened within you. It's okay. I was afraid too when I first did this exercise. But I encourage you to push pass your fears and do it anyway. Do it now.

Dear Daddy,

_____

_____

_____

_____

_____

_____

_____

_____

_____

_____

_____

_____

_____

_____

_____

Angela Carr Patterson

Chapter Four

A Father's Love

Letter writing can be very powerful. It allows for us to dig deep into our feelings and pull them out onto paper. I have found clarity about a situation simply by writing a letter to the person and then tearing it up. It's just a way to clear my head, release some pain and discover solutions.

In this chapter, I asked a good friend of mine to write a letter to his daughters and allow me to share the letter in this publication.

I wanted to include a letter from a father for two reasons:

1) I wanted the fatherless girls and women to hear the heart of a father who learned how to love and validate his daughter. Whether your father abandoned you, or perhaps he died, I wanted you to read this letter and pull from it what you did not get from your own dad.

2) I wanted those fathers who have rejected, abandoned or not been present in their daughter's life to see how a real dad shows up for his daughter. Not to bring shame to you, but to give you an example and encourage you to do the same for your daughter. I realize that many fathers never had a role model or a teacher to show them how to be a father.

If you are a woman or girl and you didn't receive what you needed from you father, I want you to take the words from this dad to his daughters and experience what a daughter mean to her father. I would even go as far to say that your father may feel this way about you, yet, he lacks the language or the skill to express it.

Maybe your father didn't know how to be father to you. We don't know what the reasons are that dads don't show up fully for their girls. But we do know that there are men who do. But just because your father wasn't there, doesn't necessarily mean he didn't care.

Perhaps the words in this letter are not spoken from you father. But they are spoken from a father.

To the fathers who are reading this book, use this father's letters as a guide for you as you begin to find a way to reconnect with your daughter. I would never refer to you as a deadbeat dad. I understand that there's a story behind every story. There's a truth behind every truth. But I say no more to the excuses or the playing the victim. This is an opportunity to tell the truth to you about yourself. Answer this question, "Am I the father my daughter need?" As you read this letter, find your own answer.

******

An intimate letter to my daughters: Konica Rochelle "Boss Lady" Avery and Tse'lani Sekoya "Mini-Me" Drew .

Okay, first of all I know you think it's a little out there for me to be sitting down and writing this letter to the two of you. You are probably looking at each other with that look you always get when I do something out of the norm and for me that's 90% of the time but I wanted to just take a few minutes and share with you what having you in my life has meant to me, and to let you know that for me the greatest word in the English language is Dad,, or as you say Pops....

I never knew what it would be like to have kids; I mean my very own kids and then God showed his sense of humor because he gave me girls, two of them. Yes I was prepared for a boy as all men are but he pulled a fast one on me and until you arrived I had no idea why. It took me exactly one second to realize that the reason he gave me your feminine spirits to take care of was because he knew that I needed to know what true love meant and how deep emotions can really get. He also wanted to teach me humility.

I need to apologize to the both of you for not always being there physically because I chose a career that took me away for some of the birthday parties, sleep overs, dance classes, etc. I figured that if I was put into a position to help save the world then, in doing so, I would also save you. So I became a soldier knowing that it would also give me the opportunity to be a better provider than my Father was, yes this was selfish of me but neither one of you came with an owner's manual or parenting for dummies book so me and your mothers were winging it primarily. So yes, there had to be some sacrifices made, I've heard that if you want something that someone else doesn't have, then you must be prepared to do the things that others won't do. And I was willing to make that sacrifice in order to be the Dad that I thought you needed in your lives.

I also want the two of you to know that you are my Sheroes, it is because of the two of you that I am still so motivated to create, so motivated to not take no for an answer, so motivated to remain relevant. You see I still need approval I guess, I still need to know that I am making a difference in your lives. I need to know that I still matter.

I see so much of me in the two of you that I sometimes find myself looking into the distance and wondering when you started to become so much like me, actually that a little scary if you want the truth.

So I want to say thanks, thanks for teaching me the definition of unconditional love and for confiding in me the way you have all of your lives. Also for knowing it's okay to tell me that "Pops you might want to re-think that" or valuing my opinion even at your current ages. You are my daughters and I worship the very ground that you walk on, I always have.

I can remember the plans your mothers and I made prior to your births and through the years how you have ignored all that we planned for and eclipsed our wildest dreams by just doing you. I remain in awe of the both of you and I am proud to have been a small part of what you have become. You are my greatest achievements and I guess I said all of this to quite simply say that I love you, and yes unconditionally. Dad

******

Now, I have an assignment for every father who is reading this book. I want you to write a letter to your daughter. It doesn't matter that you haven't been in touch with her for a while, I want you to say to her what your heart feels.

Don't over think it. Don't be afraid. Shatter your shame, remove the guilt and write your daughter a heart felt letter. It doesn't matter if she's 5 years old or 55 years old, she deserves to hear your heart speak to her.

Dear Daughter,

_____

_____

_____

_____

_____

_____

Our Invisible Cries In The Dark

Angela Carr Patterson

Our Invisible Cries In The Dark

Chapter Five

The Journey

There's not one person on this planet who hasn't made a mistake. There's not one person on this planet who hasn't hurt someone in some manner. Whether it is betrayal, not showing up or simply not being the best father or daughter we can be, we can turn these things around.

I wish that I could promise every girl who reads this book that her dad is going to change and that her relationship with her father will become all that she wants. I can't promise you that it will. I wish that I could promise every woman who reads this book that it will be easy to forgive and let go. Because it's not always easy. But it is simple and it is necessary for your growth, your healing and your future.

I wish that I could promise the fathers who read this book that your daughters will accept you with open arms or that once you've read this book, you will do the right thing. The truth is, your daughter may take a while to trust you and you may never change.

The truth is, I don't know what this book will do for you. I don't know what changes will come as a result of reading this book. But what I do know is that it is all up to you.

We all have a responsibility to change. We all have a duty to live the life we were destined to live. And whether or not your father was there to give you his provision, his protection, his presence or his praise, does not give you the right to play small in life and never achieve your full potential.

We all have to take The Journey. The Journey to love, acceptance and forgiveness. This is about healing, not blaming. Recovering self, not looking for the perpetrator, but recognizing that collectively we are all suffering, and if we are going to heal, we must all actualize the power of self-love in our lives. We must say to ourselves, "I matter. I count. I am worth something."

The Journey to love, acceptance and forgiveness is a necessary path that we all must take if we are going to live our lives free of this fatherless hollow pain. I believe there are three unique steps on the Journey that will shift you into a space of joyful living.

The Journey starts with 3 steps:

1. **Redefine Who You Are**. While we receive our identity from our paternal relationships, many fatherless daughters missed this altogether. Therefore, you must redefine who you are by retracing your life beyond your mother's womb. The bible tells us, "I knew you before I formed you in your mother's womb."-Jeremiah 5:1

It was God who created you and God knows exactly who you are. As you begin to understand that you are a perfect image in the mind of God, that you are a beautiful divine masterpiece, you will also begin to awaken to the truth of who you really are. You are not broken or damaged.

As you start living your life from this truth and showing up in the world knowing that you are protected and provided for by God, it changes everything for you. Redefine who you are beyond your fatherlessness.

Take a moment and write a brief description of who you really. The real you may be buried under all the confusion that has kept you in the fatherless up and down roller coaster. I am telling you today that you can get off.

Dads, I want you to redefine who you are too. Perhaps you have not showed up for your daughter in the way you should. Perhaps you've dropped the ball. It doesn't matter because today you get to make another choice.

The scripture that you read applies to you as well. So to everyone who is reading this, I want you to take a moment and write a brief description of who you are. Who are you as a perfect image in the mind of God?

Who Are You?

_____

_____

_____

_____

_____

_____

_____

2. **Reclaim your worth.** Rejection can cause us to feel unworthy. But we can't always trust our feelings. Our feelings can sometimes lie to us because they often times they originate from our fears. Reclaiming your worth starts by you seeing how important you are. It's not by virtue of

what you do, it's by virtue that you exist. You are a miracle and you must begin to recognize that the world needs you.

Your value is priceless and when you understand this truth, your conversation will change and you will begin to release old behaviors and patterns that no longer serve you. You will show up with forgiveness in your heart, you will show up for each other and you will show up for yourself. It's time to begin new ways of being, to enter new sacred relationships and embrace new ways of loving ourselves and each other.

Take a moment and write 2 ways in which you will begin to reclaim your worth.

_____
_____
_____
_____
_____
_____
_____
_____
_____
_____

3. **Rewrite a new narrative for your life.** Let's face it! Most of us have been dealt some pretty painful cards in life. Yet, we have a choice to allow them to ruin us if we so choose or we can allow them to be the catalyst by which we move our lives forward. The beauty of life is that you get to design your own life. What has happened in your past doesn't have to dictate your future. You get to choose what kind of future you want. I believe inside each of us is

a dream waiting to be realized. A reason for your existence, a purpose for being here and a vision for your life. Your gifts, your talents and desires are waiting to emerge from within you. And the world is waiting to experience and witness them. Our pain causes us to shut down and push the world away. But to reverse this, you must see yourself differently. You must capture a vision for your life and you must live it.

Take a moment and write down 3 things you will do to begin rewriting a new narrative for your life.

_____
_____
_____
_____
_____
_____
_____
_____
_____
_____
_____
_____
_____

Angela Carr Patterson

Chapter Six

Where Do We Go From Here?

Every girl desires to be daddy's little princess. Yet, as you can see from these letters, not every girl has a chance to experience this beautiful relationship with her father. The fact is, one in three girls will go to sleep tonight without the confidence of knowing that she's loved by her dad.

There's much research and data to support this claim. However, I believe most fathers, regardless if they are absent, unavailable or unattached to their daughter, desire to be that protector for his little princess. I also believe that he does wake up each day thinking about her and wanting to be there for her.

But for a number of reasons, too many to state right now, he doesn't know how or he's incapable of showing up as she needs him to show up. Then there are those dads who are in their daughter's life physically, but for some reason he still struggles to connect deeply with her and create the bond that she longs to have with her daddy.

So where do we go from here? I believe we all have to take the Journey of forgiveness. Without taking this Journey, we run the risk of continuing this cycle of absent, unavailable or unattached fathers and creating more fatherless daughters.

Everyone in this story must start with him or herself. Fathers must begin to forgive themselves for not showing up for their daughters as they should. No doubt that you've caused some injuries that maybe difficult to heal. Yet, you must first heal yourself.

Fathers and mothers must forgive each other for the relationships and/or marriages that didn't work. It's no longer important whose fault it was because your daughter's happiness and emotional health are what's most important. There has to be a healing between the two parents for the sake of the daughter.

Daughters the forgiveness of your fathers is going to free you in ways you've never imagined. I would like to suggest that your father injured you because in some way he too was injured. Will you allow your heart to heal? Your healing can only come through forgiveness.

We all come into the world perfect and somewhere along the way people who became imperfect taught us how to be imperfect. It's the gift that keeps on giving. Our job and our responsibility is to find our truest selves. That perfect image in the mind of God. This is how God sees us.

Therefore, as much as we want to blame daddy for our lives, we can't. We can acknowledge what has been done. We can face it and tell the truth. Even if, we don't ever receive an apology.

"Life becomes easier when you learn to accept an apology you never got."-**Robert Brault**

Instead, remember where they did get it right. For some that may simply be that they donated a sperm to the process. That's where they got it right. Where they did get it right, stand on their shoulders and bless them. Where they didn't get it right, know that you can interrupt the patterns and do it better so that your children don't inherit your pain. You can choose to forgive and get it right by being better person.

When we forgive, we release the shackles that keep our lives stuck. I want to encourage you to make a declaration to forgive. Even if you don't think your dad deserves your forgiveness, I am here to tell you that he does. In some cases he may NOT deserve to have a front row seat in your life, but he does deserve to be forgiven.

This forgiveness is for you. It's the greatest gift you can give to yourself. Un-forgiveness will keep you stuck in your pain and on a cycle of struggle and suffering. It's so pervasive. It's at the root of every imbalance that you suffer. It's the core problem that indicates that we have somehow lost touch with who we really are.

You keep yourself small by agreeing with your stories of victimization. It's time to stop the insanity of low self-esteem, stop agreeing with the statistics and the collective confusion of self-loathing and self-rejection. You are not statistic, you are an incredibly beautiful being designed to become a light to the world.

It's okay that your father wasn't there. It's not your fault and it never has been. Through the power of love, acceptance and forgiveness, you can rewrite a new story for your life. Your new love story…but this time on your own terms.

It's not only an important idea to consider, but it's imperative. It's the only way we are going to heal the family breakdown. It's the only way we are going to stop hurting each other and ourselves.

So this is an invitation to see how important it is that you love yourself, forgive everyone and begin to show up as your truest self. You are no longer invisible and your cries are no longer lost in the dark.

About The Author

Angela Carr Patterson is the CEO and President of Oasis Promotions, LLC, a Personal and Professional Development Company dedicated to building "New Inspired Leaders," for transformation and change the workplace, the media, the community and the world. Angela is a speaker, author, media personality, Global Life Strategist and Founder of the Fatherless Daughters Network.

A much sought after and highly magnetic speaker, Angela has graced numerous international platforms and stages as a workshop leader, keynote presenter and corporate trainer. Recognized for her trademark message, "I'm Not

Our Invisible Cries In The Dark

That Woman," Angela uses humor, mixed with wisdom and insight, to help women awaken the truth of who they really are, actualize the power of self-love, and unleash their greatest potential to shine in the world.

Angela is the executive producer of the upcoming documentary film, The Making of a Fatherless Daughter, founder of The Fatherless Girls Summit and The Fatherless Daughters Network. She is also the author of several books, all written in her heart warming, signature style.

With a collective reach of nearly 1.5 million people globally — listeners, readers, and viewers can capture the essence of Angela through her popular weekly Internet Radio Talk Show "Heart Secrets", her Power Zone TV Moments of Inspiration videos, and as a co-host on The Imara Woman Magazine Television Show.

Angela attended Columbia College and is a former Youth Pastor and Women's Ministry Leader. She is also a Certified Life Strategist Coach, a member of The International Association of Women in Business Coaching, and The Women Speaker's Association. Angela and her husband Bill are the proud parents of five adult children, and two lovely granddaughters. To learn more about Angela visit www.angelacarrpatterson.com

Book Angela Now!

The Making of a Fatherless Daughter Workshop

The Making of a Fatherless Daughter Workshop, created by Angela Carr Patterson, is designed to address the many ways a dad can learn how to foster a deeper relationship with his daughter that speaks to her essential needs and desires. The workshop is for any father, whether he's present, absent, unattached or unavailable in his daughter's life. Fathers will learn what happens when he fails to provide the 4 P's that every female needs from her dad and how to avoid making his little girl a Fatherless Daughter.

Presented with a nonjudgmental and non-condescending approach, Angela will speak to the heart of every father who desires to rekindle, reconnect or re-enter his daughter's life in a deeper and fulfilling way. Whether your daughter is 15 or 50 years of age, it's never too late for her to become Daddy's Little Girl. Learn More: www.themakingofafatherlessdaughter.com

Angela Carr Patterson

Fatherless Daughters and Fatherless Girls Summit

A one day event designed for women or girls to help them break though their daddy wounds and being to live the life they were born to live. Details: www.fatherlessdaughters.net

The Journey to Being Process™

Based on a ground breaking work, Angela Carr Patterson has developed "The Journey to Being Process™" to help fatherless daughters do three things: 1) Redefine who they are beyond their fatherlessness; 2) Reclaim their self-worth and actualize the power of self-love; 3) Rewrite a new narrative for their lives and create a clear vision for the future.

This is a great opportunity for your organization to gain access to a ground breaking process, powerful tools, and relevant content designed to help the women and girls within your community elevate their lives onto new levels of love, acceptance and forgiveness.

Our mission is to ignite a generation of Fatherless Daughter Advocates who will facilitate workshops/programs that will totally transform the lives of the women and girls within their communities. We will provide training and ongoing support to help you lead "The Journey to Being Process™" in a workshop format or as an ongoing program that will go beyond skills teaching to becoming a life transforming experience for both the women and girls that you serve. Learn More: www.fatherlessdaughteradvocate.com

Order Other Books By Angela Available on Amazon!

Made in the USA
San Bernardino, CA
15 October 2018